Charles Rich

Give Me Your Heart

Preparing for Eternal Life

From the Conversations and Letters of Charles Rich,
Lay Contemplative (1899-1998)

Edited by Ronda Chervin, Ph.D. 2006, 2023

En Route Books and Media, LLC
Saint Louis, MO

⊕*ENROUTE*

Make the time

En Route Books and Media, LLC

5705 Rhodes Avenue

St. Louis, MO 63109

Contact us at

contact@enroutebooksandmedia.com

Cover Credit: Sebastian Mahfood

ISBN-13: 979-8-88870-035-8

Library of Congress Control Number: 2023932385

TABLE OF CONTENTS

INTRODUCTION

How about a book for the elderly by a sage who was still making disciples in his nineties?

Who was this Charles Rich, anyhow? You may already know about him from my biography *Hungry for Heaven* or his autobiography. You may also find other titles of his books on rondachervin.com among "Friends of Charles Rich."

Charles Rich (1899-1998) was one of the most fascinating Hebrew-Catholics of all time. Born in Hungary in a Jewish village similar to the one in *Fiddler on the Roof*, Charles was noticed by the rabbis as an extraordinarily religious boy. He loved to stay in the forests to pray alone. His father joined one of the many waves of Jews who went to America to seek better opportunities. After establishing himself in New York City, he sent for the family.

This was the beginning of a very dark time for Charles. He found it impossible to be close to God in the teeming city and among the strict legalistic rabbis with whom he had to study. Eventually, he

lost his faith. He worked as a waiter by night and spent 8 hours a day at the 42nd St. public library searching world literature, philosophy, and religious writings for the God he had lost.

Eventually, Charles fell into despair and tried to commit suicide. Three times he tried; three times he failed, being rescued the last minute. Feeling even more of a failure, one day he went into a Catholic Church. Jesus spoke to him directly from a painting telling him that He was God and to trust in Him.

Instructed by the Jesuits, Charlie became a Catholic and then a lay contemplative, spending hours and hours of the day rapt in prayer. Catholics seeking a deeper prayer life were attracted to him, especially Jewish converts such as myself. Quite a number of books of his thoughts and meditations have been published.

One of Charles' most fervent disciples was Robert Hupka, a man of many gifts who was responsible for the most famous photographs of Toscanini and of Michelangelo's Pieta. Every day for over sixty years, Charles Rich wrote meditations. Robert

made xeroxes of all of these. He made audio tapes and videos. Robert also made notes of everything Charles said in conversation that he thought worth preserving. Now, after the death of both Charles Rich and Robert Hupka, I have inherited 25 boxes of these memorabilia. How delightful to find notes on old napkins or even the flimsy covers of straws with such sayings as these: "my longing is to be dissolved in Christ;" and "Now, Robert, you have written down enough to canonize you ….just practice 1/10 of it!"

What I realized when I started going through the boxes was that most of the truths in Charles' writings had a special relevance to problems elderly Christian readers have to cope with. This was because the favorite theme of the daily meditations of this lay contemplative was eternity and our need to prepare for it. Since I am now 68 years old (at the first printing of this book; I'm 84 at its second printing) and also do workshops on aging, I thought it would be helpful to select short excerpts on the subjects in the table of contents so that readers could just press a button for quick refreshment

and inspiration. Since Charles Rich loved the writings of the saints, I am including in each section some of his favorite quotations from them.

Incidentally, Charles Rich was a mystic, not a philosopher. Occasionally, his words need a clarifying word. I have supplied these in parentheses.

Ronda Chervin, Ph.D.

Afraid

General:

"Don't be afraid to be afraid."

"The grace to persevere is only given each day."

Afraid of Old Age:

"When all other weapons against the soul have failed, Satan brings the anxieties of old age with which to distress us."

"People are afraid to grow old on account of their vanity and pride, as well as their lack of faith in the things that will never have an end."

"The people of His own time said in reference to Our Lord, 'How can this man give us His flesh to eat?' We murmur in the same way when we ask

5

ourselves how God is going to take care of us when we get old."

"Only a fool would want to return to the turbulences of his early years…young people cannot have tranquility of soul on account of the nature of their passions." *(Isaiah 46:6 – 'Even to your old age I am the same, even when you hair is gray I will bear you…I will carry you to safety.')*

"We have no way of knowing whether it is good for us to be in sickness or in health, rich or poor, or whether we should stay in this life or be mercifully taken from it. What are we to do then but leave all things in the hands of God?"

Afraid of Death:

"Every human being now living will one day have to go through the passageway to heaven Christ can alone be for that human being, and it does not matter to what form of belief we adhere, whether we are Jews or Gentiles, we all belong to the human race…at the particular instant foreseen by God, we have to take leave of this life, and take

6

our place with those who have already left it...we shall then be all God has destined for us when He caused us to be born in time."

"Even at the moment of death there is no problem for the saint, since in order to render it bearable, he has but to say, 'into thy hand I commend my spirit.'"

"When we die, there will be no other place to go but to Him, it being to God we go when we die. We then return to Him from whom we received the existence we have. It is He who brought us into this world, and so it is He who will bring us out of everything that will ever happen in our lives; he has foreknown them and made provision for them like the powerful, wise, and loving Father that He is."

"Death is a welcome friend for those who love things divine."

"We came into this world in a definite period of time and so the wise man is he who is always looking forward to the day when he will be asked to depart from this life."

"How can you build a new house unless you get rid of the old house. This body has to die."

"Life is good because it ends and were it not to end it would become the greatest of evils."

"Earth is an exile, so why do we want to remain in it when we can be in Heaven?"

"Why is faith in his mercy and love not enough?"

"When God sees the soul is ready, He comes and takes it. The soul has to wait till God takes it."

"Soon we shall all be dead; that is to say, we shall be transferred from this life to the next, for that is all death is *(for those who do not reject God)*, a transformation of our being into the Being of Christ."

"We need sweetness in our lives, and that sweetness can only come with the ripeness which the maturer years bring with them. We cannot stay in this life forever, and so what does it matter whether a few more years or days have either been added or taken away from our lives? Old age is a prelude to Heaven and serves to open the gates thereto a bit wider."

"We should rejoice when we think of death and say with the Psalmist 'I rejoiced when it was said to

me, I shall enter the house of the Lord,' that 'house' being nothing else than our eternal beatitude. We do not regret leaving a life from which, sooner or later, we shall be taken whether we will or not.... God does us a favor in taking us out of this world, for He in that way gives us what we could never have had if we remained upon it...When we were children, we found amusement in toy trains, but when we grow up we realize how silly it is to want to go back to such kinds of recreation. Those in heaven look down upon us as we do on little children, for to them, our present earthly interests are nothing but the amusement of little children." *(Rich does not mean here our wholesome interests but our trivial obsessions.)*

"God is only real to people when they need him."

"The only intelligent thing a person can do in this life is to be always ready to die."

"Death is the true liberation theology, seeing that by its coming we are completely freed from all we have to put up with in the present life and is it

not said somewhere in the Psalms, 'free among the dead.'?"

(WHEN HE WAS 91)

"I don't want to pressure God to take me out of this world, but don't you think that at the age I'm at, it's time to go HOME?"

"God will always be nearby and so we don't die alone, He being with us both when we come into this world and when we depart from it."

"My heart and my mind have long since already been in heaven, and yet the body still drags itself on this earth. How I managed to live in this world with the higher part of the soul deeply rooted in another world, now seems almost miraculous!"

"We are dying all the time, so to live forever we have to identify ourselves with Him who is life, life in essence and nature, namely our Divine Lord."

"God makes use of the troubles of this life to shorten the years we would otherwise have to suffer. Can we imagine ourselves living forever with the troubles we now go through? Death came

through Original Sin. The fact of original sin is proven by the hospitals of the world, by death and the funeral parlor. There would be no need for undertakers if there was no sin in the world, seeing it was sin that brought about what we abhor so much, death with its consequent miseries… Christ will agonize till the end of the world, and all because of the wickedness of the human race and the sins men commit."

"We do God wrong when we look upon our departure from this life as anything but a sweet and sublime grace. For the Christian death is the wedding day of the soul with her divine Bridegroom, the Lord."

FROM THE SAINTS:

- St. Augustine: "This is the land of the dead."
- St. Teresa of Avila called death "that dear thief."
- St. Robert Bellarmine used to say, "Am I never going to die?"
- Ven. Francis Libermann: "Jesus and Mary do not wish to be feared; they wished to be loved."

AGONIZED

"There are so many desolating and sorrowful moments in my prayer life (1985), and this is as it should be, seeing that the closer we get to our home in heaven, the more arduous the journey to it becomes."

"The juice remains in the lemon unless someone does the squeezing. That's why God allows others to hurt us."

"Pascal said that 'Christ will agonize till the end of the world.' He will do so in the members of His mystical Body. Till the end of the world, all the details mentioned in the life of Christ will continue to be reenacted."

"You can't change the world. Christ couldn't. The world breaks the heart of its lovers. It lifts you up, then let's you down."

"If you are suffering, Christ is suffering with you. Then you become a living crucifix. The good thief was promised paradise on the cross."

"The cross leads us into the realm of experience which transcends the power of our mind to conceive, and into the mystical night spoken of by all those who were blessed to have been placed upon it."

"When you are too miserable to pray, your misery becomes your prayer."

(To a woman who wrote him that she had 'known hell' and wanted to learn how to pray)

"I, too, have known what hell is, because before I became a Catholic, I walked around the streets of NYC with the thought of suicide in mind. God has brought wonderful good out of all that, for it's the anguish that has brought me close to him – much closer than I ever thought a person could come to him this side of the grave. What is needed is patience and extraordinary faith in our divine Lord *(even on earth you will experience joy even though*

you may not believe it now.) God doesn't allow everyone to suffer as much as you because they would not be able to bear it the right way.

FROM THE SAINTS:

- St. John Chrysostom: "Suffering destroys in us the sympathy which we have for the present life."
- St. Thomas of Villanova: "Not in speech but in anguish; not in thoughts but in wounds will you find Him."

ANGRY

"People are unrealistic because they don't like the truth."

"The real test of faith is how you react when things happen to you unexpectedly."

"The minute your soul is disturbed, God cannot be in your soul."

"The moment something upsets you – drop it. When you touch a hot pot, what do you do? You drop it! You have a moral obligation. God rests only in a soul of peace. Drive out any disturbing thought with another thought, like you drive out a nail with another nail. To acquire this balance you have to work on it constantly."

"This world bothers us in proportion as the next world is unreal to us. Make the next world more real to yourself and this world won't bother you – at least not to the degree it does now. This is

the key, 'my secret' for the 30 years I have been following this principle."

"It is so easy to get ourselves steamed up over passing events and so we have to be on the lookout against the temptation to get excited over what will one day constitute a mere chimera and dream. The devil wants us to worry."

"What people need is love. They get plenty of everything else with those with whom they are brought into intimate relationship."

"Don't criticize; swallow it. If you resent someone, pray for that person, and see what will happen to you. This person has a soul. Christ died for this person."

"Christ came to make men gentle. He came on this earth to bring with Him the peace of heart and mind expressed in the Hebrew word Shalom."

"The day will come when evil will be punished and good rewarded by Him Who is goodness in essence. And so we should not be too angry when we see goodness flouted and evil held in high esteem."

BORED

"Don't be too systematic in the spiritual life."

"'Man is a mystic fact,' a great American religious genius wrote…the saints never took their being for granted…who can reach the full depths of those mysterious qualities that go into the making of a human being."

"Caring for people is the only way you can prove your love of God."

"So many find themselves tied down to a banal sort of an existence, and this is due to their lack of faith in Christ… we live in time like prisoners do in the jails in which they are incarcerated, so it's for this reason we find the Psalmist saying, 'Lead me forth from prison, that I may give thanks to your name.' (142:8) The saints thought of Christ all the time. Men make a fuss about material things, and this because they have never tasted the beauty of Christ's being.

"The time will come when the selfishly rich man will find that the money he has cannot buy eternal happiness, nor the taste thereof which begins on earth for those whose lives are ones of Christian virtue."

"My prayer life is getting dryer as time goes along, but this is as it should be, for the closer we come to God, the less excitement there is in our spiritual life. Think of the Little Flower and how dry and wearisome her days got to be as she got nearer to the shores of eternity."

"We lose interest in everything as we grow old, so the only thing left us is God, God, in a way we cannot conceive and imagine. It's hard to be detached from the great and beautiful things God has made, and so it's only in our old age we are in a position love God Himself, without and apart from, the things made by Him."

DEPRESSED

(The thoughts of Charles Rich I have included here do not relate to clinical depression requiring psychiatric treatment, but rather the older use of the word to describe disappointment or prolonged sadness.)

"When you have a legitimate pleasure you like, don't think that is unholy. You may need that pleasure."

"Don't take anything too seriously. That's the best way."

"When you are sad and depressed you cannot pray, and that's what Satan cherishes so much – he wants us to be as miserable as himself – nothing to look forward to but spiritual dark clouds and a gloomy future. You have to fight the good fight of which St. Paul speaks…in warfare we cannot expect to have nice and cozy feelings."

"There is no room for optimists in the Christian religion, but only for realists. Christ didn't promise us a lot of vain joys but only that which will render us everlastingly happy in the kingdom of His father in heaven."

"O life, life! You have been so wonderful to me, because through you I have found Christ and had I not lived, I would never have had the joy of knowing and loving His beautiful being, the being in which rejoices all the angels and all the saints."

"We should not have to have money to be truly rich; rich in the eyes of God. We should love with deep joy in our hearts; otherwise, we will miss the purpose for which we have been born. There is so much misery among men, so much downheartedness and it is all due to the wrong kinds of thoughts – they don't think of the joys of the next life."

"God has loved us from all eternity and there was never a time when this love He has for us did not exist in the Sacred Heart. The proof that we are loved by God is the fact of our own existence... How happy a mother is when the child for whom she has suffered so much returns to her a look of

love for all she has done for it. We should do the same in respect to the love God has always had for us."

"Contrasted with the eternal ages, what is this life? And yet, when asked by God to suffer some trial we get the illusory feeling that this suffering we go through will last for years to come, so that we become depressed at the prospect of having to stay in this life and endure the troubles the years will bring with them. When this happens, we have to ask for the grace to realize…that after this life will be over, all we have gone through by way of pain of body and mind will become as if they had never even been…we need to root ourselves in Christ in order to reject the dark and depressing thoughts which present themselves to the mind. …we must think more of God's holy eternity and all the blessed souls that are there – we, too, shall one day be with them."

"Look forward to disappointments. That's how you get rich spirituality. Another day, another dollar. Another day, another grace."

"We are like rubber balls pushed under water and coming up again. Don't ever stay down."

"Take the attitude in life not to expect anything from it, whether material or spiritual, thus we are developing the virtue of holy abandonment and thereby promoting peace in our souls."

"Adam and Eve wanted to know good and evil. It is not good to analyze evil which is depressive."

"The only time things will loosen up is when your soul is loosened from your body."

"Some people don't want to move on and so they look upon old age as a kind of burden. Nothing disconcerts them more than the fact that they will one day be compelled to take leave of this life, and this whether they will want to or not, whether they will be in a mood for doing so or not...In a spiritual way we have to keep going until we are safe in our Father's house in heaven, and so, until that day arrives we cannot be perfectly at ease or settle down... we should rejoice at the news of death's approach."

"'Vanity of vanities, the Preacher says, vanity of vanities, all is vanity.' In Hebrew, this word vanity

implies deception and fraud. We are deceived if we place too much emphasis on the importance of the present life and not on the one to come. Any moment of the day or hour God may send His angel in order to bring us completely to Himself."

"It is not important whether things outside of ourselves are pleasant or unpleasant, for even if they are pleasant, they are powerless to fill up the void in the soul for things of heavenly and divine which cannot be enjoyed by our bodily sight. The real satisfaction of the soul lies in the things only experienced in the depth of our being. We should thank God for natural beauty but the supernatural kind experienced in the substance of the soul is infinitely more desirable. We can have this inner beauty no matter where we are and if we don't have it we will be miserable no matter where we are. Adam and Eve were not satisfied even in Paradise, which shows only the possession of spiritual and invisible good things really make us happy."

"Optimism is not a Christian virtue. Neither is pessimism. Realism is."

"You have to blend the ascetical and the mystical. One without the other can get you in trouble."

"Happiness or unhappiness does exist in our hearts, but it has nothing to do with anything outside ourselves. When you have learned this truth and mastered it, you have everything."

"If you are not lighthearted there is something wrong with your spiritual life. God is happy and if you are not happy you are not close to God, if you were you would have some of his happiness."

"The greatest sufferings a human being can go through is to face the problems of life without faith."

"We have to be miserable in order to avoid trying to make this world our home."

"For a lover of Christ, it would be shameful to regret that life has to have an end. To look back with nostalgia is vain and cowardly…It is 'God is not loved enough for that which He is, since it's the gifts some people want and not the Giver of them.' He has always had a few loyal friends, like Job of old, for, having lost all he had…he uttered these immortal words: 'The Lord has given, the Lord has

taken away, blessed be the name of the Lord.' We should have these words in our hearts whenever something goes wrong in our lives…we cannot be gloomy and depressed if we are to carry out the task allotted to us from all eternity….God and the things he allows us to go through are above the reach of reason and so we have nothing but naked faith on which to lean and rely."

FROM THE SAINTS:

- "I do not promise to make you happy in this life but in the next, Our Lady said to one whom God loved very much." (St. Bernadette)

DESPAIRING

"To love God is all that mattered in the lives of so many saints who are now in the state of glory."

"Many people think of suicide on account of physical and mental anguish, but they pray and God gives them the grace to avert such a horrible solution…in only a few more years we will both be in heaven."

"The punishment of God is letting people become victims of their own judgment."

"If you have lost all consolation there remains the one hope to have God in the next world; to hope to have after death what you do not have here."

"God always comes to your rescue, but before he comes to your rescue, you have to be convinced that only God can help you – like the disciples in the storm."

"How can we be miserable with the whole of heaven's bliss in our hearts – we have this bliss when we have Him who constitutes the cause thereof. We should arm ourselves with these truths for they act as a charm to the calamities of this life and as an antidote to them. We take drugs when we are afflicted with some bodily disease; when the soul gets sick, we have recourse to the words of God. 'Heal me, O Lord,' the Psalmist cries out to Him who refers to Himself as the divine physician."

"There is nothing on earth which God cannot use to make us happy and give us peace – no circumstance can arise in our life in which this cannot be done, for being almighty and omnipotent, He can do the impossible. Where men see a limit, God beholds the unbounded, the uncircumscribed, and that which to Him offers no obstruction....There are no obstacles for Christ but only for men, and so it is to Him we should turn and not to them when we wish to have something done, something which requires unlimited scope. St. Paul says, 'I can do all things in Him who strengthens me.'"

DISCOURAGED

"Instead of concerning yourself with what you think you are not, just love Christ, and give him the entire love of your loving heart. He begs people to love Him, and not in the least to worry about their shortcomings which so many mistake for sins."

"God can do the impossible where men see a limit. God beholds the unbounded – no obstructions."

"It is Christ and nothing but Him that's worth desiring and coveting in this world and this infinitely more passionately than the miser hoards the gold that he can't take with him to the grave."

"How happy David must have been to have written the Psalms, especially those which bubble over with exaltation and joy. 'Be of good cheer, for I have overcome the world.' Jesus says."

"These weaknesses are necessary to convince the saints that their sanctity is not their own but God's special gift to them. If they would not have their great weaknesses, they wouldn't have realized how good God was to them in not paying attention to their shortcomings, but instead showering them with blessings."

"St. Augustine says that we should not 'promise ourselves better times.' We cannot be happy in this present life, and 'no one can.' And yet we do everything we can to do the exact opposite of what he says to us, we go to extreme lengths preparing ourselves for a life in which we cannot be happy... has anyone ever found complete and perfect happiness in the present life?"

"We sometimes get discouraged at the limitations of our mortal lot. When this happens, we have to call to mind that we have Jesus in ourselves, and having Jesus in ourselves what do we not have in that possession of Him? We are privileged to have God in ourselves and yet we complain."

"Start to think right, then you will act right. But you won't think right until you stop kidding yourself."

"Your problem is yourself. That is where all your problems come from."

"God will not ask you why you didn't succeed. He will ask you why you didn't try. There is a danger in wanting to succeed because if you don't succeed you will feel discouraged and not want to try...You can't succeed anyway. Success is for heaven. In this life we can only try to succeed."

"The closer you get to God the more you see your weaknesses. People don't see their weaknesses because they are not close to God. There is darkness in their soul."

FROM THE SAINTS:

- St. Augustine: "The wealthy do not yet have the wealth of heaven."

- "When it seemed the Society of Jesus he had founded would be condemned, St. Ignatius said 'It would take me fifteen minutes to get over it

if that happened.' How important then are failures in your life that you let things get you so upset?"

DISGUSTED

St. Teresa asked our Divine Lord: "How do you expect us to live a life as miserable as this?"

"Take care to preserve sweetness."

"All this is going to pass away, but you hurt people when you criticize them. The hurt will last. Keep patience."

"It is the sinner that needs you, not the saint. You must pray, overcome yourself, otherwise you will not want to do good any more."

"Pride is the only disgusting thing in the universe, there being nothing in it which is of a nature repellent to a human being but that only which was brought into this world by means of the devil. He, Satan, is the only being we should hate and despise."

"We cannot be happy in the present life. Saint Augustine says that no one can. And yet we do everything we can to do the exact opposite of what he

says to us, we go to extreme lengths preparing ourselves for a life in which we cannot be happy...has anyone ever found complete and perfect happiness in the present life? If he or she has, let them come forward and declare that they have. Augustine says we should not look for better times."

"Why are there so many crooked politicians in the world, so many liars, so many corrupt and evil people in it? They point out by their very depravity the goodness of those who are good and make this goodness of theirs stand out in clear bold outlines."

"Christ allows some of the saints to undergo diabolical temptations...to see the gates of hell opened in order to make them realize that it is due to His mercy and love that they do not fall into the abyss of evil, and remain in it forever after they die"

"You must convert everything into prayer, like throwing scraps, by themselves useless, into a stew and making the stew richer. Every insignificant thing – turn it into prayer."

"Try to see the good that people accomplish. See the good and disregard the little things. Make a

bargain…never let a little thing interfere with the greater good."

"The devil wants us to be dissatisfied with ourselves and to want to be different than what we are and so to make us restless, discontented, and unhappy. God doesn't care about your imperfections – they don't bother him, but you think they bother him because they bother you. But he cares about your peace of soul."

"We need wonderful human beings to counteract the devil cheapening the lives of so many people. The devil cheapens the lives of millions of people by depriving them of the opportunities they have of becoming the loving men and women it is God's will they should be."

We are not here to have peace of mind or tranquility of soul or anything else that would make us feel at home in this life and render our few years livable with a minimum of trials, anguish, and distress."

"When we get to heaven we shall thank God for everything He allowed to happen to us because we shall there see how God had drawn good for our

eternal well-being from everything he allowed to happen to us."

DOUBTFUL

(In this section, I have included some thoughts about unbelief in the faith, but others which are more general.)

"In regard to your spiritual life, you can't get to the top floor without passing through the first floor."

"The devil creates doubts, disturbances, often tempting us through complex rationalizations when simple trust and faith in God will restore peace in our souls....Give yourself the benefit of the doubt. Not to do so will allow the devil to disturb you."

"God is the easiest person in the world to get along with."

"Sin dulls in man the sense of the mystery of all things and the more this sense of mystery is dulled the more widespread does unbelief in God be-

come… a faithless age is one in which men no longer take the trouble to wonder at all things that are wonderful and for which no rational explanation will ever be possible."

"Isn't it astounding how God works…He crucifies you!"

"To get to know God in a deeply intimate way we have to suffer and there is no one outside of ourselves who can do that suffering for us; be he friend or foe."

"The crucifixion answers all questions."

"Every human being has a story of himself written in heaven. There is a book there in which every deed of his life has been recorded – a biography of himself the angels have taken down. When we leave this world we will find that nothing has happened to us without a well-conceived plan on the part of divine Providence which worked for the good of our eternal well-being…. this disclosure will become a source of joy to us for all eternity. Every minute we live is precious in the eyes of God for every minute we live we can increase our riches in heaven."

"Christ in no way had to undergo the pangs of death. He chose to do so out of love for us. Is there any great and lasting thing in this world which has not been brought about by the pain and misfortune of some human being?"

"Why remain perplexed when there is no need for such perplexity? We have but to become saints for that perplexity to be completely removed. By becoming united with God we will be given the grace to experience the joys of heaven even while we are still in this life, and experiencing these joys we will get to know what heaven is like."

"We are so prone to rationalize and look for answers to questions that were never meant to be given in time. A whole eternity awaits us in which we shall be given to understand what we now believe. The saints were not impatient with God for they knew they will know in heaven what is now so baffling to them. The little man, the man of small mind and circumscribed comprehension, want to know everything. Show me, he says, demonstrate the undemonstrable. What a beautiful thing it is to be able to believe and not to want to understand

what it is God's will we should now accept on faith alone. Generous and large-hearted souls believe and that is why they see the glory of God. Those who are unconfiding miss the beauty of their existence for by means of their pettiness they fail to perceive the mystery."

EXHAUSTED

(written when he was 91)

"In addition to the weak spells, I feel nauseous all the time, and so weak when I get up that I have to go back to bed, not once but many times during the day. I used to spend a whole hour in thanksgiving after Mass, but when I go to the chapel I can't stay more than a few minutes due to my being so tired...I don't want to stay in this world even for one minute longer than God will call me to do so."

"Every time the hot summer comes around I get the feeling that as a result of the health I'm in, I will not be around for another year of it, and here I am still around in a 99 degree heat. But, as there is an end to everything that exists in time, there will be an end of the life I now live and I'll soon be home

with God...The heat may turn out to be the greatest of blessings if it facilitates my going where we will be happy in the way God has intended for us to be happy for all eternity."

"We see ourselves disappearing little by little for just as the drops of water ultimately wear away the rock on which they fall, so little by little the body that is ours reverts back to the dust out of which it was originally fashioned. It is only the soul that is immune to this law."

"There are times in our lives when the conviction imposes itself upon us that nothing matters but Jesus and Mary, but not Jesus and Mary as their names are to be found written down, but as the personalities of them are infused into our souls by the Holy Spirit Himself, for it is only when this takes place that any real help can come to our poor, weary-laden, and distracted souls."

"I am not only hungry for heaven, I am getting starved for it, for it's getting so that I cannot walk a few blocks without becoming exhausted."

"Life means struggle. If you don't want to struggle, you will lose what you have."

"Your problems accumulate like dust. Train yourself not to take on responsibilities that are not necessary. In (trivial) matters, it is not important that you do or don't do them."

"It's hard to talk of heaven while still on earth, and yet glimpses of its bliss continue to find their way into our weary-laden lives."

GRIEF-STRICKEN

(at leave-taking)

"In some marvelous and ineffable way we are now already the way we will be in heaven, loving that in each other which we will take with us when we leave this world, our deep inner being. And, loving that in each other, we can also have each other, though we are separated from each other physically."

(after visiting the grave of his dear holy friend Tom Prendergast)

"Bernic and I stood on his grave, and we were overcome with a holy kind of envy for his soul, because that soul of his is now completely with Christ,

and in that completeness which he always wanted so much."

About a friend Charles wrote a few years before his death, "There will always be (this friend) for me to love, her essential self cannot pass away because it is mingled with eternity."

"God has given us two different modes of communication, one with the living, one with the dead. The dead speak to us and we to them, but we do so in the depths of our being which God alone is able to penetrate...there is a certain deep-seated satisfaction whenever we think in a holy way of those who have already left this life."

"No one ever came to Christ unless his heart was broken."

After the death of Mike Sweeney, one of his disciples, Charles wrote, "Mike appeared to me today, and he looked right at me, as if he was alive, and he is alive, existing in Him who is Life Itself...he seemed to want to say something to me which he felt I could not understand...showing there is a kind of wall separating the living from the dead which will exist until we will be with them in the

state of glory...that the souls of the faithful departed exist in Christ is confirmed by these experiences of them that now and then come to us.... something of the other world is made evident to us when we feel that someone who has left this world shows himself and herself to us...these experiences are shrouded in mystery...but it was vivid and real, making me feel it was the soul of Mike looking at me, and not just some kind of false vision and chimera... these are glimpses, tiny glimpses, seeing if we get the full flush of them we could not go on living, the joy and delight they bring with them, forcing the soul to take leave of its bodily habitation. For Mike Sweeney the battle is over, and he won the war, the war we still have to keep fighting. How lucky he is as are all those who already are safe with God."

(about the death of a holy man)

"We should grieve for those who die, but we should do so in a Christian way and not a pagan manner...we should have a spiritual and super-

natural joy, the joy they have who have lived and died the way our beloved friend died."

"It is God's will that when we hear that someone has died we should feel the loss as keenly as we can, for does not St. Paul say we are members of one another...Hard is the heart of the man who is not compassionately affected by the sight of someone who has died. We are all in need of God's compassion and kindness in the way that we are all subject to the same sad end...How can we help being affected by the sight of a fellow human being brought to nothing by death?"

"What is death but the best friend any human being is able to have, since by means of it, he is freed from the many miseries of his life and ushered into the joys of the world to come. It is a delusion to dread that which we should love more than any other thing."

"We should moderate the sadness we feel when we learn that someone has died by the thought that he has taken a part of ourselves with him...part of us has emigrated to heaven every time someone by means of death goes there ahead of us."

"A saint said that God sometimes gives us our purgatory on this earth, so in losing your son and husband you must have gotten yours. We want to see God immediately on our departure for this life, and so, Ronda dearest, God loves you very much so He will give you the grace to be with and see Him…it is a special sign of God's love to suffer so much."

"As we advance in years, people leave us, and this is a blessing, since we have more time to be with God."

"'His and her soul is mine not yours,' God says to those He takes by means of a holy and happy death. We should in no way complain in that those we love go back to God from whom they came…"

FROM THE SAINTS:

- St. Margaret Mary, "In the next life, God's friends will see all they want of each other."

GUILTY

"There is only one misfortune and that is in the depths of the heart, the sinner knows what this misfortune is; it consists of the sin in him, this and nothing else. Christ came to redeem us from this sin and that is why we love Him so much."

"We should in no way distress ourselves over the sins we commit, but instead turn ourselves over to the mercy of God."

"We hug our sins and our miseries, and we refuse to give them to God who alone knows what to do with them, and so it's in vain that He came down from heaven to take these sins and these miseries upon Himself. 'You have not yet given me your sins,' our Lord said to a saint, and He says the same thing to us because we don't want to give them to Him, and we keep them for ourselves. He does not want us to carry our sins on our poor, weak and small mortal shoulders."

"There would be no sin in the world if there was no pride in it…the sin of the flesh being the direct result of the sin of pride, and we are allowed to sin with the body because and only because we have first allowed ourselves to commit the sin of the mind… *(For instance, not having the humility to trust that God will give us His happiness one day, and therefore thinking we have to seize what would seem to make us happy right now in sinful ways.)*

"Great sinners are afraid to trust God. It takes great sanctity to trust Him. So, if great sinners trust God they become saints on account of their trust."

"We can never be devoted enough to the Passion of Christ because of the sweet soothing consolation we derive from it…Were it not for the sufferings of Our Lord, there would be no Church in the world today and consequently no means of redemption from our sins…the wounds of Christ are the last refuge of the sinner, said St. Bernard."

"Would God have become a human being were there no sins to be atoned for by His becoming a human being? We do not know, but sin exists, so it has to be atoned for, and we make this atonement

49

by means of everything that God allows to happen to us...the final atonement made for sin is the death we are allowed to go through. So we welcome whatever pain we will be allowed to go through for such a purpose."

LONELY

"What loneliness and unhappiness there is in human hearts! And this is due to the fact that Jesus does not constitute their center."

"It's getting lonelier and lonelier, so I am led to read of the saints saying that they too felt this loneliness, including the great St. Teresa."

"The life we have to go through can indeed be lonely, hard, and cruel at times and the heart-breaking anguish in it almost more than we think we can bear. At such times the only thing we can do is set our eyes upon the Cross."

"Isn't the Blessed Sacrament enough for you? Do you need so and so as well?"

"The world is filled with marvels for those who love God, and it's no lonely place in which to be. How often do these celestial spirits become our

close companions and friends. We need but have pure hearts to perceive them present in an invisible manner."

"You can lose everything else, but you can never lose God."

"You cannot depend on a human being. The only one you can depend on is God. There is happiness in this life, but people make the mistake of depending on it."

"You are not here to please people. You do have to perform acts of charity, but charity does not always mean to please people – sometimes it does, but not all the time."

"You have God but you also have to have God's friends. You can't do it alone."

"To be united with God you must be alone. Others can help you along only to a certain point; then you must be alone. God must teach you how to pray. There are no two persons alike and there are as many ways to God as there are persons."

"If we don't stick together we have no opportunity for charity."

"God is jealous. He tears us away from every-body except Himself and when He tears something – it hurts."

REBELLIOUS

"The Devil says 'kill time,' because time, if it is not killed, can be used for spiritual advantage."

"The devil does not want you to be a saint, that's why you go through what you do, you'll never be free till you get to heaven. Many saints had worse temptations and God allowed them…we have a facility of picking out from the New Testament what we think fit to follow and leave the more humiliating aspects of the life of Christ to our theology books, to be read and studied but not followed."

"You have a cross. You mistake your cross for a problem, so you try to solve it. But it can't be solved. That is your problem!"

"The cross is the bread and butter of spirituality."

"God could take all your troubles away instantly, but you wouldn't have God. The condition for having God is the troubles!"

"We all have to suffer, but when you have the faith you have help."

"How you accept the circumstances in your life determines the progress of your spiritual life."

"The hardest thing is to accept things as they happen to you. Don't blame circumstances… blame God… God works through those things."

"The reason why you or anyone else who loves God very much suffers is hidden deep in the Bosom of the Godhead, and you will know the reason some day; the day of eternity as it says in Scripture. Here you are not asked to understand why you suffer but to believe that nothing unjust can occur to you by the hand of an infinitely just God *(Charles doesn't mean that nothing is unjust but that God can bring good out of it)* …Look up at the Cross and commune with the figure of Our Lord upon it. Ask him why you suffer, and He will answer you by saying why did I suffer?…Suffering can, if we so will, procure for us the grace to become co-redeemers,

sharing in the love of His own Sacred Heart…The greatest blessing in this world is to be able to have something to endure out of love for Him who is love."

RESTLESS

"To be a great artist you must know when to stop. One additional stroke might spoil everything. Without a brake, a car is no good. If you keep on speeding, you'll wreck yourself."

"The punishment for not going to God is that you have to go to everything else that is not God. Happiness can only come from doing the will of God."

"God help you if you are ever satisfied in this world."

"It is in thinking of Heaven that I expect to find peace of soul and in nothing else."

"We wish to become beautiful with the beauty of the God-Man and to possess if only in a finite degree some of His own prerogatives...we have a longing in our hearts to be in His Image...there is a craving in us to be both immortal and beautiful

with the immortality and beauty of the God-Man, for we realize that it's only in that way we can ever hope to be happy both in this life and the next. We want what the holy angels already possess."

"It's good to feel ill-at-ease in a world like this, in which nothing remains the same from one moment to the next – everything in it is in a state of transition and the flux of which the Greeks have spoken."

"'How canst thou wish us to love a life as miserable as this,'" St. Teresa said to our Divine Lord, and I feel that these words are among the most beautiful ever spoken by a human being. They express what's in the hearts of everyone whom our Lord has given the grace not to feel at home in this life, but to want to be in the heaven of the life to come."

SICK OR DISABLED

"The devil does not want us to accept pain in the right Christian way, for he knows that if we do so, he will lose all influence over our lives. Christ came to teach us that suffering is sacred...properly borne, pain wins eternity, and to lose our soul is to reject the cross.....Pain is bitter, but it cures the soul of all its diseases...one reason we sin is due to the fact that we do not want to suffer."

"'He who made me is now unmaking me,' a saint said as she lay dying. On our way out of this life, we will receive the grace to be remade in our divine Lord, so that thus remade, we will no longer be the limited and finite human beings we now are...we, too, shall one day be the kind of men and women who are now in the state of glory."

"I have always had a great devotion to the Risen Body of our Divine Lord as well as the resurrected bodies of all those who love Christ. We will all of us be extraordinarily beautiful, and so we can afford to grow old and misshapen for the few years we are here on this earth."

"To be sick is to die before death arrives, for... sickness acquaints us with eternity by showing us the true nature of things of time, for in no other way could we see through their deceptive quality...we are undone by sickness and made over into another individual...though prayer is good, to suffer is infinitely more important...we feel our own helplessness and realize that it is only through the goodness of God that we don't end up in despair...sickness is a test of how much we love things that cannot end with time."

*(writing about his holy friend Tom
who was an invalid most of his life
and was getting worse)*

"He (Tom) made a contract with God to live only for His holy will, so he is prepared for everything that may be God's will for him, no matter how painful and humiliating this may be for him."

(Letter to Joan Kondracki (3/26/92)

"There are so many things in this world which are so difficult to bear and to endure in a Christ-like way, such as suffering and disease and even the pains of death. This world, not being our true homeland, God does not see anything wrong in His allowing us to go through the troubles with do on this earth…the Psalmist says to us: 'I am a foreigner on this earth.' We are all of us foreigners on this earth, so it's for this reason we find so many things on it which are directly opposite to the way we feel they should be. St. Paul tells us that we 'have a house not built by hands into which the sorrows of this life will not enter in.' So, it's for this reason all the saints looked forward with so much genuine joy to their one day being with Christ in the state of

glory, and that St. Paul proclaimed that he 'longed to be freed from this life and to be with Christ.'"

"We should not fix our gaze on what the eye can see in ourselves (our bodies) but only on what is discernable spiritually...It does not matter how we look from without as long as we are well within. "If it was good for you to feel better, God would make you feel better, wouldn't He?"

"So much emphasis is put today on physical well-being that we are inclined to forget the importance of suffering in our lives and the great need there is to bear that suffering with the proper Christ-like dispositions. And while it is all right to take care of our health of body, still, we must remember that that is not the reason why we have been put on earth. We have been put on it in order to sanctify our soul, so as to make them ready to meet the bridegroom when He comes...In His eyes, it is Heaven that counts and not these few pain ridden paltry earthly years."

"If you lose your eyesight *(something he was threatened with),* God will give you something

more beautiful than what you could see or read in a book."

"Before we leave this life, all the gifts we have received from God will have to be relinquished, and we will be stripped of all we had. As we grow old, the senses of our body decline, and we finally lose them altogether. There is nothing we can hold onto in the present life save God Himself. It is humiliating to realize all this, and that is why so few accept old age and death graciously. In due time, God takes away the gifts He gave us to restore them in an infinitely more perfect way in our life in Heaven. …Referring to his death St. Paul said (2 Cor. 5:4) that he did not want to be unclothed but to be 'clothed over.' To be 'unclothed' is to be compelled to part with the things that made this life so enjoyable, such as the senses of sight, hearing, taste, and touch. As we advance in years, we lose the capacity to do the things we enjoyed so much – it's moving-day – when we grow old, and this is never a pleasant prospect to have to face….we should offer up the inconveniences of old age in atonement for sin. God would never have permitted us the

humiliation of growing old if there were not very special graces attached to such a process."

"In a way, it is easier to endure pain than decrepitude, for in pain, there is nothing to humiliate us – for in pain by courageous bearing of it...we develop a spirit of fortitude and with that a consciousness of our worth. People admire us when they see us bear pain with Christian resoluteness. God could have so made us so that we would not have to grow old. However, in his infinite wisdom He foresaw its necessity to counteract our tendency to pride...when we see ourselves decline, we cannot be proud of ourselves, and so we turn to Him *(in our helplessness)*...The devil tells us that old age is an evil and so we should reject it. He dreads the profit to our souls the advancing years will bring with them. There is a devilish pride in those who fail to base their lives on the truths of faith and the rejection of old age is a manifestation of such pride."

"As a result of our decrepitude, let the world cast us off; God will be there to pick us up...with old age come graces that are infinitely sweeter

(than those of youth). Youth is harsh and intolerant and it is unforbearing…. We should thank God we are growing old since each day we grow closer to the place of our heart's desire…we should say with St. Paul 'even though our outer man is decaying, yet our inner man is being renewed day by day.'" (2 Cr. 4:16)

"Sickness and misfortune are our friends, for they remind us that we shall soon be freed from our present confinement in our mortal state."

"Every time we say the Our Father, we say 'Thy kingdom come,' and this means that we pray for death since it is only after this life is over that we shall fully enter into the Kingdom of heaven and not until then."

"God has given us exterior and interior riches and so, when one of these passes away and becomes ineffectual, we have that within ourselves to take their place….There have been saints who had within themselves that for which they would not exchange for all the wealth of the world, spiritual and interior good things, those enjoyed by the angels and saints in heaven…Yes, there is a world

within ourselves and that world is in no way dependent on the health of the body, nor the use of the senses. 'The kingdom of God is within you,' Our Lord says, within and not without. When we grow blind, we see things on which the eyes of the body were unable to look since the vision of them transcended the capacity of our corporeal nature. What beautiful things the poet Milton saw when he lost the sight of his bodily eyes? He has given expression to them in his famous masterpiece *Paradise Lost*. We should in no way despond when God allows us to grow ill and lose the capacity to enjoy ourselves in a physical way since He has a way of compensating us for this deficiency in His own divine way. The whole of Scripture is replete with mystical hints of the glorified state of the body we now bear about us, and so the reflection upon this is a source of joy to the soul."

WORRIED

"How can anything that now happens in this life in the least way disconcert us. It cannot do so on account of the hope of heaven's joys that is in our hearts…how can we give way to the despair they have who do not have such a grace."

"The rosary takes you out of time – like going out of the city into the country."

"Nothing is worth worrying about. You can always have God – day and night."

"If you are doing all the worrying, there won't be anything left for God to do."

"We have to learn that others have a cross to carry and realize that we cannot take it from them. Leave all to God's unfathomable mercy. St. Peter was freed from fetters through the ministry of the angels…until then one must continue bearing quietly those chains that are still one's portion. The

more quietly we do so the less we feel them. After all, one must not meddle with the angels' business! …Usually one gets a heavier cross when one attempts to get rid of an old one."

"It is important to go to God Himself for advice. It is our free choice to come to Him. If you have peace you have everything you can desire."

"There is no real security in this life, and so we must take refuge in God in order to attain it. He is our safety and protection…the days go by and we along with them. Soon, they shall be no more and then where will all the problems be which tormented us so much? They will be annihilated and be as if they had never been."

"I have never met a person who didn't succeed in solving the problems of his life in thinking of Jesus with faith, hope, and love."

"You can't worry and trust God. If you have faith you don't worry. If you worry, you don't have faith."

"Most of our troubles never happen. They come in the imagination. Therefore, we must restrain our imagination."

"We make our own miseries. God wants us to take it easy."

"We worry too much about the future of temporal things and that is a serious mistake – we cannot be here forever, and so we are forced to heed the words of a recently deceased poet when he tells us that we should 'have no home in time.'"

"Faith is the privilege of not having to solve all our problems."

"You are not allowed to worry. If you do, you are disobeying God."

WHO THE SAINTS WERE

"The saints are like so many spiritual eagles who soar above that which can be seen, heard, touched, tasted, and felt by the senses of the body. …We are so prone to hobble along where it is God's will we should soar and fly. Our Lord came to set the soul free from the limitations of this life and render it independent of them. In a spiritual way, we must move out of the restrictions of time and take up our abode in the great Beyond that Our Lord is."

"The saints alone yield up to Christ the love of their whole hearts."

"We have to love Christ with intense passion and ardor for otherwise we will be led astray by the beauty with find in things beautiful; God loves us passionately and so why should we not love Him in the same way."

"We have to have the courage to say God wants me to be and to do what nobody has ever done or been before."

"While some fall in love with another human being, the saints fall in love with Christ."

"If we are not saints, we better become saints before we draw our last earthly breath…for we are here to get to heaven."

"In the words of the prophet Isaiah, 'God's hand has not been shortened.'…He keeps on making great saints of those who would otherwise be content to remain just good Catholics."

"People are afraid of God, and this is because they don't love Him enough. If they would love God, they wouldn't be afraid to ask Him for the graces to become as great a saint as those who have lived in past ages…Can you say that God is not good enough, and powerful enough?"

"People become saints by way of the cross. It has embraced your dear person and enshrined you in Christ. Has anyone ever become one with Him save in the way and manner of the Cross?"

"When we look at a saint, we see Christ. The sight of a saint takes us out of ourselves, and brings us from the mortal to the immortal. We cannot express in words what we see in the face of a saint, for

it has an indefinable quality, something like God Himself and reflects His own glory. Saints are given to refresh us on our journey to Paradise – they bear about them a fragrance from heaven: 'We are the odor of Christ,' Saint Paul says in reference to all the saints…there is something in the expression of his (the saint's) face which does not originate in time. The face of a saint soothes the soul…How fortunate we are to be able to look at an actual photograph of those who have been so close to Christ!…We should surround ourselves with portraits of saints, so that by looking at them often enough we will be able to absorb into our souls some of their own beautiful qualities…by looking at them with devotion, admiration, and love, we also pray. We should have a holy envy of their virtues and strive zealously to become what they have been….to love God as they have loved Him, a spur for us to scale their own heights."

"The saints were the most colorful and most fascinating human beings to be found in this life, for they refuse to settle for anything that's less than the infinite."

"Is it not God's will we should all of us becomes saints, seeing that every man and woman and child…can, if he or she wishes, become as great a lover of Himself as those in the ages gone by."

"Most of the saints thought they were flops. Just try to do your best."

"The saints were never able to understand how anyone can fail to know what God is like since there are evidences of Him in every existing thing… There is enough beauty in the creatures to break our hearts with love for Christ to whom they point, whom they signify and symbolize."

"The only problem a person has is to be completely oriented to God because when you are completely oriented to God all your problems are solved."

"Prayer is an occupation which begins on earth and lasts for eternity. That's why it is the most important occupation in all the world."

"Detachment from human loves is necessary at the beginning of the spiritual life. After becoming perfect God draws good from everything and you can love all things."

"The saints were not too much concerned whether they derived any satisfactions from their relationship with God – for them it was enough to know that they have given themselves completely to him."

"What the priest writes about, the saints perform and the saints are not content to write a poem but to be one. The saints are the dreamers of true dreams and true visions."

"There is no greater gift than a holy person who accompanies us on our journey to heaven. You are such a person, that's why you mean to me all that you do."

"God demands all before he gives himself to you."

(about a holy Jesuit priest, Fr. W.F. Clark)

"There was an air of exaltation about his whole being, you were made to feel that he lived and moved in realms such as only the blessed inhabit...there was a holy rigor about him, but it failed to depress, and the austerity of the rigor was

more consoling and more heartening than all the softest qualities found in other men...Fr. C. evoked hopes and longings which only prayer can stir up, so that to be with him for a time was like being close to God...I was tempted frequently to let him know how I felt about his great wisdom and learning. Yet, I dared not so much as hint at it, for he wouldn't have been pleased...I asked him what places to avoid in order to lead a more perfect life and he replied: 'avoid all places where you don't hear the word eternity mentioned frequently.'"

...His whole life "The saints looked forward to death every single moment of the day and it was for this reason they were happy men and women. We must imitate their example if we wish to have real peace of heart...the peace Our Lord spoke of when He said, "My peace I give to you."

"How important it is to have friends to help save and sanctify our souls. Without the aid of others in this direction, we will find ourselves to be at a considerable disadvantage. We cannot stand alone in the spiritual life, and this no more than the soldier in the field of battle...The longer we live the

more we realize that it is due to the encouragement we receive from others that we are spurred on to fight the good fight of which St. Paul speaks…We are too weak to stand alone….This life is not easy to be in and without understanding hearts and minds, almost impossible to bear….A cry will always go out from the hearts of the saints calling out to their friends for sympathy and love….We cannot disassociate ourselves from our fellow men, since they form part and parcel of our own make-up, there being no strangers in the eyes of God… there is a mystical body and it's our incorporation into it that makes us Christians and pleasing to God's Divine Son…The Church has His sacraments, and so we have to hold on to them in order to be saved, saved, that is, for an eternity of joy. Is it not a kind of madness to live on earth as though we will remain on it forever? And, aren't the saints the only wise ones who live on this earth as though they may to get off it at any moment."

FORETASTES OF ETERNITY

"There is a sweetness in the saints that gives us a taste of what heaven is like. A saint once said 'God is a sea of honey.' St. Thomas said we could never have enough pictures of Christ which show His sweetness."

"It is possible that in many of our dreams the angels of God give us a fore-glimpse of the wonders that await us as soon as we wake up from the sleep the present life is."

"I never saw anything so beautiful as the face of the Blessed Virgin sculptured in marble by Michelangelo, and yet, as I looked at that beautiful face, I realized that beautiful as she is there depicted, she is infinitely more than Michelangelo conceived...we cannot understand how Beethoven could have written the 5th symphony....how Dante could sustain the 'word-

music' of the Divine Comedy, for genius inhabits a world all its own and differs radically from the one in which the generality of mankind move and live and have their being…on earth, we gaze with rapt awe at so marvelous a work, and as we do so, our hearts and minds are lifted up into the sublime and beautiful world of heaven."

"It is only those who have affectionate natures who are capable of experiencing all the delight divine things have in them. Few know God to be pure Beauty, pure Truth, and pure Love. Many know God all right, but they do so in a merely theoretical and abstract way; a way in which it is insufficient for them to make Him the mainstay of their lives…not enough to set their souls afire and to be consumed thereby."

"What I love in you cannot grow old, and it cannot change, it is a foretaste of heaven…Why people don't ask God for the grace to love each other in a supernatural way is one of the mysteries which will be made clear in heaven, and it's so sad that they do not love each other in this way."

"In order to know what heaven is like, you have to pray for the grace to have some of its quality in your own self. When we look into ourselves, we see a depth we cannot fathom…there is something in us that doesn't belong to time."

"By means of sublime dreams, God gives us a taste of the joys awaiting us in the life to come."

"What an amazing thing the love of one human being is for another, and what an utter nothing is the earthly love for that human being compared to the one we shall have for him in the life to come? Do we ever think of the kind of love we shall have for each other in the life to come…freed from the limitations which in the present life surround that love?"

"Everything on earth is only a symbol and metaphor. We live in a world of signs for what exists in heaven."

"To know what heaven is like, we have to pray for the grace to have some of its quality in ourselves – there is no other way its joys may be experienced while we are still on earth.…what is heaven but a state of bliss for which no other word can be found?

What is heaven but a state of being to which the laws of geography do not apply? Heaven is not something to be understood by our feeble intellect because the nature of it transcends anything we are able to conceive...the Jews of old referred to heaven as a 'land flowing with milk and honey' into which the mystical Moses that Christ is would one day bring all those who by the lives they led have become worthy of entering into it..." *(If there were not these riches within us Jesus would not have said)* "The kingdom of heaven is within you." Heaven is close by, closer than we are to our own selves – its nature and essence constituting the highest region of our being. We do not have to ascend upward; we have but to enter deep within ourselves, and we will certainly find it there."

"We would like to know by personal experience what heaven is like, but the best way this can be done is to contemplate all our Lord is both body and soul. Was He not a kind of heaven when He moved among men? ...We shall never be able to get a better idea of what heaven is like than by contemplating all Our Lord is. What is the Sacred Name of

Jesus but another word for heaven. By loving Him we get a taste of the joys of heaven."

"Our whole problem in this life is a question of love. As we grow older, this love for the right things becomes more purified and refined, and this is why interior things are such a joy to the soul – the soul that knows no old age and which is rendered fresher and more vigorous with the passage of time. As we draw closer to our home in Heaven, the happier we become and the less distance there is between that in ourselves and that for which we have always longed so much – beatitude."

"Contemplation is getting lost in God."

"How long can we live a life which is always reminding us of its brief and transitory nature: only yesterday, someone we loved very much passed away, and today, someone else, and tomorrow it will be the same story. Life is quick to exact its toll of those who thought they would stay on earth a long time."

"Eternity is for being mystically awake and so it is not without reason that the life we are now in is referred to as the night and the one to come as day."

"If the relationship we have on earth is the source of so much happiness, what will the one be we shall enjoy in heaven? We both live for the things of the next life; that is why we get along so well – we both want no other life than the one Christ is."

(Probably written to a holy
Sister Adele Marie who was dying of cancer)

"You yourself shall soon be in Heaven and when you get there you will pray for your dear companion in all that's holy. How pitiful it is to have nothing to look forward to beyond the grave and to be limited to the present life! How fortunate Christians are, because for us there is another dimension, the one Our Lord Is. You and I live in this dimension and it is this which gives our lives so much meaning and significance... The saints in heaven are with each other in a way quite different from the one on earth... you are something more to me than just another human being – you become something I cannot completely fathom, some sweet

and wonderful mystery I shall completely understand only after this life is over. We are all mysteries…As the Psalmist says 'I give you thanks that I
am fearfully, wonderfully made.' (Psalm 13:14?)
…We are all fearfully, wonderfully made, and so
we should have this in view all the time we think of
ourselves or some other person with whom we are
intimately bound up… Friendship provides us
with the opportunity of sharing ourselves with
someone, first, Christ, and then His members...
Heaven will consist in the sweetness we will derive
from being close to God and we can get a taste of it
on this earth by being close to Him here."

"The sea takes you out of time and helps the
soul to think of eternity which the almost limitless
stretches of ocean water resemble."

"If we look back at our childhood days, we will
quickly find traces of the atmosphere of heaven."

"People look forward to a vacation. Why not
look forward to heaven. It is a grace for which we
must ask."

"My prayer is getting lost in God."

"Though every human being and everything natural are great and good things, they are surpassed infinitely by what is divine and what is supernatural."

"*(when I think of my spiritual friend)* a consolation from heaven enters my inner being, flooding that inner being with a joy and a happiness which has its roots in another world, the world of love, truth and beauty in which we shall both be after this life is over."

"We would like to know by personal experience what heaven is like, but the best way this can be done is to contemplate all our Lord is…Was he not a kind of heaven when He moved among men? Does He not still continue being that same heaven right now? Do we not feel that He is when we reflect upon Him with devotion and love? It's hard to talk of heaven while still on earth, and yet glimpses of its bliss continue to find their way into our weary-laden lives."

- St. Bernard assumes us that 'the soul of every just person may be truly called a heaven.' (Sermons on the Song of Song.)

- John of the Cross: "Creatures are the crumbs fallen from the table of God and which serve to whet the appetite for the divine good and beauty Jesus is."

- St. John of the Cross: "The soul lives where she loves more than in the body she animates; for she does not live in the body, but rather gives life to the body, and lives through love in the object of her love."

THE LONGING OF

THE HUMAN HEART FOR GOD

"How sad it is to think that the hearts made for love fail to turn to the only source which can fill up the need for that love? It is to Christ we must have recourse if we wish to be genuinely happy and to him only... How disappointing creatures are when contrasted with the good Jesus is! How pathetic is the effort men make to fill up their hearts with all that Christ is not and how frustrating and disappointing such efforts are."

"We thank Thee for being Jesus, that is, for being a Savior to us...for a favor from heaven it is, not only to believe in our Lord Jesus Christ, but also to be able to love Him with a Love that will last throughout the eternal ages, for, what are we going

to do, throughout these eternal ages, but to have the grace and blessing to love our Lord and Savior…who has made evident the love He has for us, by His creating us out of nothing…do we ever thank God for is making us out of nothing?'

"We have been asked not to depend on creatures, not because they are not good…everything God has made is good, but because of their limited and circumscribed nature. Creatures are not everywhere available, but God is, and so when we need a friend most he may for all kinds of legitimate reasons not be around. God alone is always dependable…always around…God has created the good things in this life for our use, but for absolute dependence we have to go to Him who is everywhere and always present. We must love our friends, but to depend upon them all the time is not what God wants us to do."

"Christ is joy; He is beauty itself and sublimity and above all, He is the divine delight in which we shall become immersed after we have the grace to enter into another and infinitely more beautiful world than the one in which we now find ourselves;

and being what we are, sojourners in a foreign country; we cannot but look forward to this delight as we do in nothing else."

"We shall, throughout eternity, revel in the beauty of Christ's being, and we shall there revel in the love in Himself we will then be given the grace to have."

"I would like to write a book with the title *Dare to Love* because it takes daring of soul to love that which is divine in itself…people are afraid to let go of their hearts with the love they have for God and for each other."

"Christ alone can give us that which will make us happy for all eternity, namely, freedom from the many miseries to which we are now subjected."

"Heaven is the natural home for souls like ours, and it is there our hearts should be centered…not on earth with its imperfect way of experiencing the divine."

"I am anxious to get out of this world so the scope of my activity may increase."

"It is not spiritual exercises that make you holy but the grace. The exercises dispose you for the grace."

"In saying: Let Him Kiss me with the Kisses of His Mouth (The Song of Songs), the soul prays to be penetrated by the spirit of Christ and impregnated by His being. The kiss is symbolic of the action of the Holy Spirit, which takes place in the substance of the soul: for among the different degrees of union with God we can attain in this life that denoted by the kiss is the sweetest and most sublime of all. After passing through the different stages of the spiritual life, the soul realizes there exists a state higher than all, and it's for this it asks when it says "Let Him kiss me with the kisses of His mouth."

"He mystically is ourselves by being the being of our being and the love of all things lovable."

"Prayer is the longing desire for the divine."

"Both cannot co-exist. One must die, God or I! That is the terrible thing about the interior life. Unless you are dead, you cannot be a saint."

"True prayer is longing for death, the more ardent the longing is, the better we pray."

"'Set my soul free from prison,' the Psalmist prays, 'that I may praise thy name.' We cannot adequately praise God in the present life, and so this constitutes a strong motive for wanting to be released from it – we wish to be there where this can be properly done, heaven and there only. To be fully with God we have to die, there being no other way in which can enter into perfect relationship with that which is divine…By allowing us to die, God takes away from us a good that is finite to give us one that is infinite."

"We will have in Christ all created good things, and so nothing will then be wanting to the soul which it now finds so necessary to have."

"There is a phrase in the Sacred Scriptures with a haunting quality about it and it runs like this: "Be prepared, O Israel, to meet thy God." Now by 'Israel' is meant every human being who genuinely loves God and whose main concern in this life is to look forward with joy to being with Him in heaven."

"We are heading for Heaven; earth is departing, and the years that pass away are the vehicle that's

taking us there...With bated breath we long to be Home with God....We cannot answer a lot of questions this side of the grave, but we will know when we pass the boundary line which separates time from eternity."

"The saints regarded each other with a holy kind of awe, and if we were as holy as they, we would do the same thing."

FROM THE SAINTS:

- St. Bernard: "We cannot now form an adequate idea of the capacity for love which the soul will have in the next life."
- St. Therese: "I thought I was going to die and my heart nearly broke with joy."

GENERAL

(Here I have added quotations from the writings of Charles Rich that are not directly related to aging but that I found important in themselves for anyone to read.)

St. John of the Cross spoke of the body as "the small house that the soul is in."

"Jesus is not far off. He is right here in the midst of us. He is in our inner being."

"Art, philosophy, and science are without power to assuage the pain that's in our hearts… without the holy Catholic faith, I would be the greatest pessimist and would die of despair and boredom."

"Time is a vehicle on which we are borne to eternity."

"People don't want the Truth because truth means sacrifice."

"I practically spend my whole time in looking up the key words from 4 different Hebrew lexicons

in reference to the book of Psalms. I carried a copy of the Hebrew Psalter in my pocket when I was only 5 or 6 years old. Though I didn't understand the words, I enjoyed reciting the Psalms for their sheet musical quality and out of reverence for the fact that they are divinely inspired…I find this kind of activity the ideal way of preparing my soul to meet Our Lord."

"To be happy in this life, you have to pray for the grace to always be able to say, 'Come, Lord Jesus.'"

"The world goes along its own sweet way of delusions and dreams, and it refuses to think of the utter fragility of our present existence."

"We stand in need of many things as we go on living; but these needs begin to diminish with the passing of time. We find we can do with less and less of the satisfactions to be had in the present life. Every moment we live is a grace from God. There are as many graces in our lives as there are moments in them, and even seconds. The soul lives by grace in the same way as does the body by the air we breathe."

"Be content with the good things of the present life, the forces of evil say to us, but leave heaven alone and never give the joys there awaiting us a single thought…Christ beckons us, but He has a rival along this line, so great skill and great divine wisdom is necessary to know to whom to give up the love of our whole hearts."

"It is not words which will save our souls but the Body and Blood of the Redeemer of the world. It is the adoration of the flesh of Christ that enables us to bear the trials of our earthly lot."

"God needs people in order to dwell in them. We were born to be a dwelling place for almighty God…take away this reason and there is no basis left for the existence you have…so live for Him alone."

"Jesus! Jesus! Jesus! We shall for all eternity pronounce these holy words and it's in the pronunciation of them that our happiness will in that eternity consist, though we even in this life derive joy of heart and mind from the pronunciation of the Most Holy Name of Jesus."

"We thank God for every day we live, seeing every day we live we can thank God for His giving us that day to love Him and each other in Him, with the Love Itself He is."

"You are what you want to be."

"By prayer is not meant the mere use of words, but the lifting up of our hearts and minds to a Good that is above ourselves, as well as the realization of our eternal destiny...that can be jeopardized by the commission of sin."

"Even from a purely literary point of view the Psalms excel anything ever composed by a human being, be he a Homer, a Dante, a Shakespeare, or a Goethe. No nation has produced anything compared to them, and so they will always remain a unique gift to the human race by the people of Israel. St. John of the Cross before he died said 'we shall say Matins (the early morning psalms) in heaven,' indicating that the time will never come when the Psalms will not be sung even in eternity."

"If God were a master poet, what sort of verse forms would He have written? The Psalms... to recreate our hearts... the Jews sang the Psalms on

their way to Jerusalem *(city of peace)* and so, like them we sing psalms. To the believer in Christ Jerusalem is a term to denote the vision of peace after this life."

"You've got to pray or you are finished! If you don't pray you are lost. You lose your relationship with God."

"The devil is more clever than you are."

"He *(any of us)* doesn't pray; he says prayers."

"God gives graces only in proportion to our wanting and asking for them."

"You cannot sacrifice the Creator for any creature."

"People don't remember what you said but the kindness of you."

"When you meet a human being, the first thing you have to recognize is that he (she) has a soul that will last forever."

"Each day we live serves as a step to eternity; that is why each day we live is a grace from on high."

"We shall all grow old, and we shall all die, and so this consideration should serve to make us all brothers under the skin."

"There are a whole host of things we are unable to do with the lessening of our bodily strength. However, there are an infinitely more important of them we cannot accomplish when we are young – we cannot be as compassionate and kindhearted, as forgiving and understanding. Youth carries many illusory notions about itself and *(one)* of these is that the world can again become a Paradise. As we grow older, we become more realistic along these lines, and so we no longer look for a heaven on earth – in the words of St. Bernard, we ourselves long to become a kind of heaven."

www.ingramcontent.com/pod-product-compliance
Lightning Source LLC
LaVergne TN
LVHW011409080426
835511LV00005B/447